Green Sapphires

Green Sapphires

BookLeaf Publishing

India | USA | UK

Presentation by *BookLeaf Publishing*

Web: www.bookleafpub.com

E-mail: info@bookleafpub.com

ISBN: 9789363307605

First edition 2024

To mummum, wherever you are!

A Farewell Letter to Love

Farewell, love—you are too hard.
You ask for too much.
I am empty now,
Farewell, go find another heart.

I gave for too long, hoping you'd return,
But you never came when I needed you most.
You felt special because I made you so,
And you thought I was just a host.

My heart aches;
Now I know why it's called heartache.
Nothing feels as bright
As it did at the start.

But I guess that's how it is meant to be.
It will always be less, always a compromise.
It will always be about surviving,
And will end with that feeling of saudade.

Silence

People talk about the music of the woods,
I hear the silence, profound and still.
It grows around me, slowly engulfing,
Overwhelming, it claims my will.

If only I could explain,
Silence heals, just like a tune.
It doesn't need creation; it simply exists,
Present by day and under the moon.

It separates you from the world,
Yet keeps you firmly in its embrace.
It makes you want to lose yourself,
To become as endless as its space.

Silence soothes and calms your mind,
Striving for connection, both near and far.
It's abstract, intangible, like the wind,
Not stored or written, just as we are.

You breathe it in but can't give back,
A cycle complete, a peaceful track.
Silence is the end of the cycle of giving,
A serene path to continue living.

Love's Labor Lost

When I was a little girl, I thought love was rare,
Only seen in movies, a dream beyond compare.
As a teenager, love seemed just a way to pass
time,
Nothing felt permanent, all just a fleeting rhyme.

In college, love seemed a gift for others, not for
me.
I wondered if I was worthy, if I could ever be.
But then I met you,
You made me feel so special, so true.

You didn't speak much, but you showed you
cared,
With your gaze and presence, you always were
there.
You listened to my dreams and my pains,
In return, I thought you shared the same.

But now it's all different, and things have
changed,
You don't need me now, your feelings
rearranged.
I feel like I'm a convenience, here when you're
alone,

Did you love me only when you had time to
own?

Our lives should have been different, it seems,
Not like everyone else's, but lost in shattered
dreams.
We had our own love, more intense, more bright,
But now it's just convenience, no longer the
light.

We shared stolen glances, touches, and more,
But it feels like you've closed that door.
What was once special now seems so routine,
It's all become a matter of convenience, not
what it once had been.

Breaking and making a masterpiece

Every day I break a little, cry a little, soothe a little.
They say I am strong, that I have weathered worse.
But why don't I feel so?

I cry today because hope is lost.
Life's anchors seem washed ashore,
Or maybe drowned in the ocean,
Far from my sight.

Am I breaking my old self or making a new one?
Whatever emerges will be a new me.
"Is that bad?" they ask.
I don't know, but the process surely hurts.
If the new me is better, was the old me not enough?

What is enough? What is my worth?
Is the new not truly the same as the old me?
Stone and sculpture do not have the same worth,
But they share the same matter.

Change isn't required, but growth is beautiful.
If you feel the itch, let it guide you.
You might become something you never
dreamed—
A new creation, worthier and whole. A
masterpiece!

The battle within ourselves

And when the sun shone, I realized more about
myself than I had during the long night.

The grass shimmered like a green carpet,
And the trees were the embroidery,
patterns scattered with villages and forestry.
The high peaks appeared like brown and white
buttons.
If only someone could weave me a dress out of
them.

With the sun and the frost,
the world spread its warmth and chill in the air..
together.
It mirrored the battle in my mind.

What is this world if not full of opposites?!
The high mountains and the low oceans,
The cold snow and the hot sand,
The green grasslands and the barren deserts.
The world is like us; and we are like the world.

We all have good and bad within us.
No use separating Jekyll from Hyde.
We are young and old at the same time.

We work for love and for money,
We need words and we need music.
Without either, we cannot have a song.
Without one, we cannot find the other.

Within me, the battle continues,
But I learn to live with it.
Everything will fall into place in its own time.
When I finally write the book of my life,
The plains and peaks will be equally important
in the topography.

Limits

Is there a limit to rising?

People grow to a certain height and then stop,
Plants and trees also have their bounds.
Apple trees halt at a few meters tall,
While pines can reach eighty, but even they
cease.

Is it nature's law that we cannot surpass
The limits it places on us?

But look at what humans achieve:
Buildings soar higher each day,
Technology evolves, soon to surpass us,
Human civilizations endlessly advance.

We've outgrown every other species for
centuries,
Refusing to bow down.
We speak of the future and, in time,
Will envision futures beyond our reach.
There is no limit to where we can go,
To what we can achieve.

Nature might set limits on us,
But we need not!!

Dreams

I dream of clouds, I dream of rivers
Sometimes I dream of trains whistling by
There are dreams so vivid, and dreams so
blurred
And then there are dreams in which I can fly

Sometimes I dream the whole world is ending
And sometimes it's rising from the ashes of the
last
My dreams keep me dreaming
And hoping things to be better than in the past

In some, I dream you were still here!!

Laughing and talking, sitting close with me
Sometimes you are complaining
Of the same daily mundane things
Your rigid opinions, so frustrating

Yet how I wish I could still live those moments
again
How i wish that maybe -
If I dreamed long enough and hard enough,
That it might actually be true!
Oh, how I wish I could dream so through!!!

A fractured Inheritance

When I was a child, I believed everything you
said
You were my first teacher and my first friend
I learnt from you the alphabets and the numbers
You taught me to write, to pray and to abide

You said day, and the nights became days
You said to go on, I went on even I wanted to
stay

You never let me quit, You had too much at
stake
You were living through me, trying to do what
you couldnt!

Thank you for your dreams!
And thank you for the attitude
Your hopes and your failures,
I carried them both alike!

Yet what I could not carry was the life you lived
by
And the lights and the darkness that those times
occupied
I hope one day I can make better sense
Till then, I carry this fractured inheritance.

What comes after Love!

What comes after love?
My little one said,
He looked at me,
But I stared ahead.

We love our family,
We love our friends,
But what comes after,
When all love ends?

Or does it?!

Love has many forms,
That of a Parent for a child,
For a pet or a puppy,
Or a best friend who's wild.

But is there a love,
That outweighs all those?
A love that goes beyond,
And will never come close?

What comes after love?
He asked me again,
Everybody loves me,
But is it all the same?

Then it occurred to me,
Not all love's made equal,
And what comes after,
You have had all others?

It's the love that,
I felt then for him,
It fills my heart each day,
It's called a mother's love.

The light inside you

If ever the colors seem to fade away,
Or the sparkles leave your eyes,
Just take a long look inside you—
You'll find them nearby.

There is magic within you,
With fairies and butterflies,
And heroes who save the day,
With their friends and allies.

Seek the light within you,
Let it shimmer, let it shine.
If you believe you can make it happen,
The whole world will be thine.

Your mind can take you places,
Your heart can show you where,
And that little star that guides you,
Will always be there.

Trust in the dreams you cherish,
Let your spirit freely soar.
With the magic that's inside you,
You can always find more.

Ruhi

When Ruhi came to me,
She was just on a piece of paper,
An idea, a sketch from your imagination!

Eight years later,
We got a baby boy,
But where is that little girl,
The one we seemed to enjoy?

Ruhi, you are still there,
At least in my heart,
A lovely echo from the happiest
Days at the start.

When love was new,
And our ideas were wild,
When the world didn't matter,
And we acted like a child.

You will always be a part of our lives,
I might never see you,
But you are the most beautiful piece
Of my heart, that's true.

You were the symbol of young love,

You were the best part of your father,
You could definitely beat your brother,
And be my partner in laughter.

I know you are there, in some parallel world,
And I still love you so, my darling little girl.

Growing up in love

When we met, we were kids
Two newly minted notes
Two bricks just out of kiln

We still knew not much
Of the world and its twists
We had just lived in home
We were not afraid of the fists

Two decades later
As we look back on the story
It's a story of two birds who have now learned to
fly

We have grown up together
We have built a world of our own
It has its pains and sorrows
But it's still love up to the brim!

A life well lived

At the sunset from my window
I look dreaming of days gone by
It's been a long 67 years
It might be time to say goodbye

Has it been enough?
Too long or too short
Where should I end
Or should I restart?

My world has changed much
From the days I just dreamt
There have bad days
But I have a whole bunch of the best

Dear world, as I close
The curtain of my life
I hope you will remember
A woman who never shied away from a fight.

Death and the Living

Death is inevitable,
All-ending and true.
No one escapes its grip,
It's where we all go, me and you.

But death is for the dying,
Not for those left behind.
For us who remain,
It leaves a wound unkind.

"Life is for the living," they say,
Yet death haunts us too,
For how can I face the day,
Without thinking of you?

How can I live my life,
Without your laughter's ring?
Or miss the harmless banter,
That could sometimes sting?

Death is scarier for the living,
Not for those it takes away.
It makes each passing moment,
A longer, darker day.

Keeping you near

Not strong enough to keep the promise,
Too sad to keep the smile in place.
Too much, too little—it was all the same,
As I stood beside you in that fateful space.

I sang all night as you fought your last fight,
Some called me crazy, some looked in despair.
But how could I stop? How could I be quiet?
Singing was all I could do, my only air.

I've never felt as helpless as I did that day,
All my resolve and focus washed away.
Had to keep a face to keep others contained,
But who was there to wipe my tears away?

Sometimes I recall your every small detail,
And sometimes I wonder how little I knew.
I go through days thinking of you at every turn,
Hoping it doesn't send me spiraling through.

You are still so present, in my heart, in my talks,
And in every single thought I bear.
When will this end? Or do I want it to?
My last desperate attempt at keeping you near.

Immortality

There was a time when I thought
It'd be good to live long,
To be immortal and
Witness everything, right or wrong.

But as I enter
Another decade of my life,
I wonder if it's worth it,
To grow old and live to ninety-five.

As I continue to live,
And people start to pass by,
The pain and the hurt
Keep my heart occupied.

As I grow older, I don't want to be old,
I don't want to live long, just big and bold.
Immortality's definitely not on my list,
If a Genie comes along!

Hapiness

Happiness is the dream of yesterday,
The success we find in today.
The promise of what lies ahead,
The joy for which our lives are led.

Happiness is parents when you're a kid,
Friends that you grow up amid.
It's love when you find your partner true,
And your child, carrying a part of you.

It's part of the happy ending
That you find in your partner.
But it's not an ending,
It's just the start of something new.

Happiness isn't a goal to chase,
Nor an end that we must face.
It's what we live with every day,
More than what we live through on our way.

My mother, my friend

A plaque above my table says—
"Always my mother, forever my friend!"
That you were, and it will always be true.

You were my passion,
My hopes came from you.
To change the world together—
That was our dream come true.

You left, I let you,
Not thinking how hard it would be.
Now every moment is a burden,
Sometimes too heavy, thinking of you.

You are my mother,
You will always be so.
As long as I am alive,
Your love will forever flow.